THE GREAT TRAIN ROBBERY

HISTORY-MAKING HEIST

true crime

THE GREAT TRAIN ROBBERY
HISTORY-MAKING HEIST

by Brenda Haugen

Content Adviser: Philip Edney, Public Affairs Specialist, Federal Bureau of Investigation, Washington, D.C.

Reading Adviser: Alexa L. Sandmann, EdD, Professor of Literacy, College and Graduate School of Education, Health, and Human Services, Kent State University

COMPASS POINT BOOKS
a capstone imprint

Compass Point Books
151 Good Counsel Drive
P.O. Box 669
Mankato, MN 56002-0669

This book was manufactured with paper containing
at least 10 percent post-consumer waste.

Editor: Brenda Haugen
Designers: Tracy Davies and Gene Bentdahl
Media Researcher: Marcie Spence
Library Consultant: Kathleen Baxter
Production Specialist: Jane Klenk

Library of Congress Cataloging-in-Publication Data
Haugen, Brenda.
  The Great Train Robbery: history-making heist / by Brenda
Haugen.
     p. cm. – (True crime)
  "A Capstone imprint."
  Includes bibliographical references and index.
  ISBN 978-0-7565-4360-0 (library binding)
  1. Train robberies—England—Buckinghamshire. 2. Thieves—
England—Biography. I. Title. II. Series.
  HV6665.G7H38 2011
  364.15'52094259—dc22   2010017722

Image Credits: AP Images: 27, 29, 30, 50, PA Wire URN:6204261,
46; Getty Images, Inc.: *Daily Express*/Hulton Archive, 43, Dennis
Oulds/Central Press, cover (top), Dennis Oulds/Central Press/Hulton
Archive, 60, *Evening Standard*, 34, 55, Files/AFP, 75, Keystone, 37,
Michael Fresco, 81, Popperfoto, 9; Mary Evans Picture Library, 70;
Shutterstock: flavijus, cover (money bag), Lightphase Photography,
cover (train), 1, SVLumagraphica, cover (ax)

Visit Compass Point Books on the Internet at *www.capstonepub.com*

"YOU WON'T BELIEVE THIS, BUT THEY'VE STOLEN A TRAIN."

Few crimes are so shocking or so terrifying that the stories of what happened live on years, or even decades, after the offenses occurred. The shock waves from these crimes often ripple beyond the areas where they happened, fascinating and frightening entire nations—and sometimes the world. Some of these crimes are solved. Often they are not. But even when the cases grow cold, the evidence remains and awakens the amateur detective in all of us.

TABLE OF
CONTENTS

8   Surprise Attack

16   London's Criminal Element

22   Planning the Crime

32   The Heist

40   The Plan Breaks Down

52   Capture and Trial

64   Life on the Run

78   The Robbers' Fates

88   Timeline

92   Glossary

93   Additional Resources

94   Select Bibliography

96   Index

CHAPTER 1

SURPRISE ATTACK

W hen the Royal Mail train unexpectedly stopped on the tracks in the middle of the night, the six postal workers in the High Value Package (HVP) car weren't alarmed. Maintenance on the railroad tracks was commonplace. However, the noise they soon heard outside the train car was anything but ordinary.

"Get the guns!" they heard a man say.

The postal workers hurriedly began piling heavy canvas bags against the door. The sound of breaking glass interrupted them. A large masked man holding an ax tumbled through a broken window into the car.

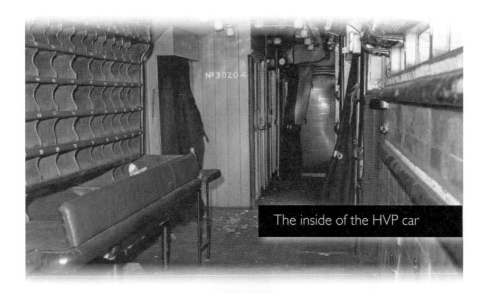

The inside of the HVP car

TRAVELING POST OFFICES

In 1838 the British government established night mail trains across the country. Delivery time for letters and packages was shortened because workers sorted mail on the trains as they traveled through the night. Workers dropped off bags of sorted mail at each destination and picked up new mail. The largest night mail trains had six sorting carriages, 11 letter and package carriages, and more than 50 post office workers. Important letters and packages were routinely stored and sorted in one special HVP train car. In 1936 the government sponsored a short film about this system. *Night Mail* became a famous documentary. In the 1960s traveling post offices were still widely used in England. New technology, however, later decreased the need for the special trains. The last British night mail train completed its route in 2004.

Just moments before, the postal workers had been busy sorting mail. The HVP car's wooden lockers were stuffed with 68 white canvas bags full of cash. The workers had crammed another 60 cash bags into a narrow space between the lockers and a sorting table.

The mailbags piled against the door didn't keep other men from coming into the car. Wearing overalls, ski masks, helmets, and gloves, they pushed their way into the compartment. They carried ax handles and blackjacks. The criminals struck Chief Sorter Frank Dewhurst and Post Office Inspector Thomas Kett, then forced them and four other postal workers to lie on the floor. Two robbers stacked the moneybags while several others formed a line and handed the loot off toward a waiting truck and two Land Rovers. Each bag—in all they weighed about 2.5 tons (2.3 metric tons)—was so heavy that one robber pushed and rolled them toward the truck rather than carrying them.

The daring heist took place August 8, 1963, near a quiet country lane in Buckinghamshire, England, at about 3:30 a.m. At Sears Crossing, about 40 miles (64 kilometers) northwest of London, the robbers stopped the night mail train on its regular route from Glasgow, Scotland, to London. Scottish banks regularly sent old and extra paper money to their London branches on this train. August 8 was a few days after a legal holiday and weekend. Because of that, the train car containing high value packages carried more money than usual.

The robbers took about 120 sacks filled with cash. The bags contained more than 2.6 million British pounds (about U.S. $7 million). At the time, it was the largest amount of cash ever stolen in England.

After about 25 minutes, one of the robbers shouted, "That's enough!" Even though seven sacks remained to be loaded, it seemed that the robbers' schedule was more important than getting more money.

BRITISH CURRENCY THEN AND NOW

Since the value of money usually grows over time, the 2.6 million pounds stolen in 1963 would be equal to more than 40 million pounds today. In U.S. money today, the loot from the Great Train Robbery would be worth about $63 million.

In 1963 British paper money was printed in several denominations, including 10-shilling (half-pound), one-pound, and five-pound notes. The five-pound notes came in two sizes and colors. In 1957 the British government began to replace the extra-large white notes with smaller blue ones. But the changeover wasn't complete at the time of the August 8, 1963, train robbery. The white five-pound notes stolen by the train robbers caused problems for them. The white notes were easy to spot.

"... DON'T MOVE FOR 30 MINUTES, OR IT WILL BE THE WORSE FOR YOU."

Train driver Jack Mills and his assistant driver, David Whitby, who had been handcuffed together by the robbers, were brought to the HVP car. The masked men told the drivers to lie next to the sorters.

"We're leaving someone behind—don't move for 30 minutes, or it will be the worse for you," one robber threatened.

The criminals then raced for their getaway vehicles. As they left the scene of the crime in the dark of night, their vehicles' headlights showed a money bag that had fallen on the road, but the robbers didn't stop. They sped away, past lush green grass and fields of ripe corn. The peace in the countryside was in sharp contrast to the violent theft that had just occurred.

Who were the train robbers? Why and how did this group of more than a dozen men plan this history-making heist? And how did they intend to get away with the cash?

CHAPTER 2

LONDON'S CRIMINAL ELEMENT

L ike many members of the train robbery gang, Bruce Reynolds was no stranger to trouble. The tall, spectacle-wearing man was smart, though he rarely put his smarts to good use. Instead, he enjoyed planning crimes.

"This was the part I loved—the plotting, the intricate mind games to second guess the police, covering all the angles," he later wrote.

Reynolds was the leader of the Southwest Gang—criminals in that section of London. In time he became the leader of the group that robbed the night mail train that August night in 1963.

Most of the train robbers had grown up in poor London neighborhoods. Many of them began committing crimes when they were kids. Charlie Wilson was only 10 years old when he was first arrested for theft. That was during World War II (1939–1945), when London was being bombed by German airplanes. The Blitz, as the nightly air raids were called, damaged many stores and homes, opening them to thieves such as Charlie.

HE WAS A GOOD GUY TO HAVE ON YOUR SIDE IF YOU WERE PLANNING TO COMMIT A CRIME.

Some of the robbers had become friends and associates as teenagers. For a while Wilson worked at a fruit and vegetable market with Jimmy Hussey and Tommy Wisbey. More typically, though, the robbers had become acquainted through criminal acts. That is how Wilson met Reynolds, Gordon Goody, and Ronald "Buster" Edwards. Reynolds met Ronald Biggs, then 20 years old, in 1949, when both were locked up in the same prison.

In the late 1940s and early 1950s, crime was a way of life for London gang members in their teens and 20s. Sometimes these young criminals stole cars. Roy James became known for his skill as a driver. He could make quick getaways.

Other robbers had different skills. Short, plump Buster Edwards was well-liked as well as smart. In 1963 he was the leader of London's Southeast Gang. Like clever, joke-loving Charlie Wilson and daring Gordon Goody, Edwards was known and trusted by other London criminals. Goody, who was tall and muscular, was sometimes called Footpad, an old-fashioned word for a violent robber. But some called him Footpad because he looked so dangerous. He was a good guy to have on your side if you were planning to commit a crime.

Before the train robbery, Reynolds had pulled another large heist with Goody, Wilson, Edwards, and James. In November 1962 they stole 62,000 pounds (U.S. $173,600) from an armored vehicle at a London airport. James drove their getaway car. The robbery made headlines, but the loot—an airline's weekly payroll—was less than they had expected. The criminals were eager and confident. They were ready for a bigger challenge. The idea of grabbing a lot of money in a special train robbery appealed to their wallets and their vanity.

OTHER GREAT TRAIN ROBBERIES

Train robberies-real and imagined-fascinated people long before August 8, 1963. Nineteenth century robbers such as Jesse James are legends in the American West and elsewhere. In fact, the first storytelling movie made in the United States was a short film titled *The Great Train Robbery*. Edwin Porter directed it in 1903.

In Britain the theft of gold bars from a London train in 1855 was originally called "the great gold robbery." But American author Michael Crichton called his best-selling 1975 novel about the crime *The Great Train Robbery*. He understood the broad appeal of the title.

Did a mysterious criminal mastermind plan the train robbery? The first person to write a book about the caper thought so. She even declared that she knew who this "uncrowned intellectual king of the underworld" was. For several years the public believed this tale. Now most people do not. A detective who investigated the crime later called the idea "of a 'Mr. Big' behind the whole thing … rubbish!" A historian has pointed out that Reynolds, Wilson, Goody, and Edwards were "four capable and experienced [criminals who] could have worked out the entire thing right from the beginning." According to Reynolds' autobiography, that is what happened. The career criminals used loot from the airport heist to fund their grand idea.

As the train robbery plans solidified, small-time crook Ronnie Biggs, florist Roger Cordrey, and other men new to major crime became part of the plot. Reynolds and his crew began to fine-tune their scheme.

CHAPTER 3

PLANNING THE CRIME

Bruce Reynolds lived up to his nickname The Major as he planned the train robbery. According to most accounts, Reynolds set goals and assigned tasks for the caper with military precision. At first he depended most often on Buster Edwards, Charlie Wilson, and Gordon Goody.

Reynolds may have gotten the idea for the history-making crime through connections he made after other brushes with the law. A lawyer named Brian Field—who helped defend people accused of crimes—may have put Reynolds in touch with an unidentified man who knew a lot about night mail trains. So the man, who was called the Ulsterman because of his Irish accent, might have first suggested the robbery. Regardless, it was Reynolds who figured out what it would take to carry it out.

The robbers would need a foolproof way to stop the train. They would need to find the best location for the robbery. They would also need vehicles to carry away the loot, a hideout, and enough men to complete each part of the plan. It took about seven months to make all these arrangements.

To stop the train, Reynolds turned to Roger Cordrey. A middle-class florist from a London suburb, Cordrey had huge gambling debts. He had already taken part in minor train robberies to pay off debts. Cordrey used the public library to learn about the railroads' automatic signaling system. He figured out a way to trick the system, which signaled train drivers using green lights (for go ahead), yellow lights (slow down), and red lights (stop). The lights hung beside the tracks. Before the robbery Cordrey opened boxes containing the lights, covered the green ones with a glove, and attached electric batteries to the red lights. This simple trick fooled train drivers into stopping for what they thought was an official red light. To work on the night mail caper, Cordrey wanted 10,000 pounds (U.S. $28,000) right away, plus a share of the loot. Reynolds and his associates accepted Cordrey's demands.

Reynolds and Goody told Buster Edwards and Tommy Wisbey to scout out a location on the train route for the heist. It needed to be within easy driving distance of London, have signal lights, and be far from inhabited buildings. There also needed to be a little-used road nearby to make loading the loot easy and the getaway quick. The men used special maps—called ordnance survey maps—that contained such detailed information. They took trips into the country to confirm what the maps showed. Bridego Bridge appeared to be a perfect site for a robbery.

Less than a mile (1.6 km) from the Sears Crossing signal lights, the bridge was only 15 feet (4.6 meters) above a quiet lane. Near the bridge was a private, rarely used parking area for fishermen. It was large enough for two getaway cars and a truck. Woods on one side of the area would hide the vehicles from passersby. During the next few weeks, Reynolds and his crew made many trips to this area. They noted how often trains passed through. They observed how long it took for trains to slow down for a yellow light and to stop for a red light.

Roy James had the job of learning about the train's brakes and controlling its engine. He studied *The Railwaymen's Handbook*, a guide for railroad workers. James got more information by pretending to be a schoolteacher. After he told a train driver that his students wanted to learn about trains, the man invited James into the engine cab and demonstrated all the controls. But Reynolds and others believed that a professional train driver would be best. Chance led them to one.

Reynolds' old acquaintance Ronnie Biggs earned his living as a carpenter. He had recently worked for an older man who drove locomotive engines. This man—later known as "Stan"—had given rides to Biggs' young son, who loved trains. Biggs mentioned this to Reynolds one evening at a restaurant. It was a lead that Reynolds could not pass up. He asked Biggs whether, for enough money, Stan would drive a train being robbed. Biggs replied, "For a few thousand [pounds] he'd drive a spaceship." Biggs was right. When Reynolds contacted Stan, he was thrilled. He agreed to join the caper. Ironically, Biggs, who later became the most famous member of the train robbery gang, was included in the heist only because he knew Stan.

Lawyer Brian Field helped Reynolds and his brother-in-law John Daly find a hideout. Leatherslade Farm—less than a half hour's drive from Bridego Bridge—was for sale. It seemed ideal. The nearest neighbors were a half mile (0.8 km) away, trees hid its buildings on two sides, and it had a view of the road. The main house had four bedrooms. There also was a garage and a workshop for their equipment.

Leatherslade Farm, the gang's hideout

Field asked a former client, Lennie Field (no relation), to be the front man for a minor crime. Lennie agreed. Apparently, neither he nor lawyer John Wheater—Brian Field's boss—knew anything about the planned train robbery. Yet through Brian, they helped Reynolds begin the purchase of Leatherslade Farm. The robbers moved to the farm as planned on August 6. They knew that August 8's night mail train would be carrying extra cash.

A former British soldier, James White, had arranged for the vehicles. With help from Reynolds and Wilson, he had stolen one Land Rover (an off-road vehicle), and bought another one and a used army truck. White also bought other equipment, such as a police-band radio, walkie-talkies, and handcuffs. Since the robbers planned to stay at Leatherslade Farm for up to a couple of weeks, White stocked food, dishes, and utensils. Dozens of eggs, cans of beans and tomatoes, loaves of bread, and huge tins of tea and coffee were among the supplies. Reynolds also tossed in a Monopoly game. White drove everything to the farm before the robbers' arrival.

Wanted men (clockwise from top left) Bruce Reynolds, James White, Buster Edwards, and Charlie Wilson

At a signal, a glove was used to mask the green light and a battery powered the red light.

Each man knew his part in the operation. Reynolds would be on the track well ahead of Sears Crossing. When he saw the train, he would let the others know by walkie-talkie. Daly would use Cordrey's trick at the first signal box, changing its green light to yellow. Cordrey and James would make sure the next signal beamed a red "stop."

James and an unidentified robber later referred to as "Bill Jennings" would separate the engine and first two cars, including the HVP car, from the rest of the train. James would have already cut nearby telephone wires. Jimmy Hussey and Bob Welch, both petty thieves, were there as needed manpower for the heist. Some of the men would target train workers, while others would break into the HVP car to get the loot. Some would remain with the truck and Land Rovers. Then they would work together to load the money bags into the getaway vehicles.

Human nature, however, interfered with the careful plans. The robbers may have been betrayed by a member of the gang or someone else who knew of their plan. Whether or not anything this dramatic happened, ordinary events and emotions helped foil their scheme. One thoughtless remark, not understanding country people's ways, and simple physical distress—all led to the capture of many of the robbers.

CHAPTER 4

THE HEIST

As the night mail train from Glasgow to London approached Sears Crossing early in the morning of August 8, everything seemed to be going smoothly. With everyone in place, the gang members watched the train move toward them. As planned, they used a false signal to trick engine driver Jack Mills into stopping the train. Obeying the red light, Mills brought the train to a standstill.

The 58-year-old driver stayed in the diesel engine cab. The 26-year-old assistant driver, David Whitby, climbed down to use a telephone at the signal to find out why they had been stopped. When Whitby reached the phone, he discovered the line was dead. As he was returning to the engine

"IF YOU SHOUT, I WILL KILL YOU!"

The scene of the crime—a train waited on the embankment above a country road the robbers used.

to give Mills the news, he saw a man walking toward him. Whitby figured the person was either a signalman or someone else from the train who wondered why they had stopped. When he walked over to talk to the man, Whitby quickly realized his mistake. The man pushed Whitby over an embankment, where two masked men grabbed him.

"If you shout, I will kill you!" one of the men threatened.

They held Whitby on the ground near the stopped train. Whitby, his voice shaking, agreed to cooperate. It was about 3:30 a.m., and still dark.

Back in the engine cab, Jack Mills was struggling. A masked man carrying an iron bar had climbed into the cab. Mills tried to push the intruder out, but a second masked man came to the intruder's aid. Mills later said, "I was struck on the back of the head four times, twice on the side of the head and I was severely bruised upon the upper part of my body and head. ... They had all got staves [wood sticks] in their hands and one had a piece of iron piping." The robbers later claimed that Mills' worst injuries came from his fall during the struggle. Whatever the cause, the attack led Mills to spend three days in a hospital. He needed 17 stitches for cuts he sustained. The cuts bled into Mills' eyes as the robbers forced him to drive the engine and the first two cars. Less than a mile (1.6 km) away, at Bridego Bridge, the robbers told Mills to stop.

Before the robbery Chief Sorter Frank Dewhurst and his four assistants had been working in unusually tight quarters. Post Office Inspector Thomas Kett was also in the HVP car. None of the men suspected what was about to happen, even though the train had stopped. Unscheduled stops and starts were routine. No one had ever robbed a night mail train before. The workers had no idea that the engine and first two cars, including their car, had been disconnected from the rest of the train and had moved down the track alone.

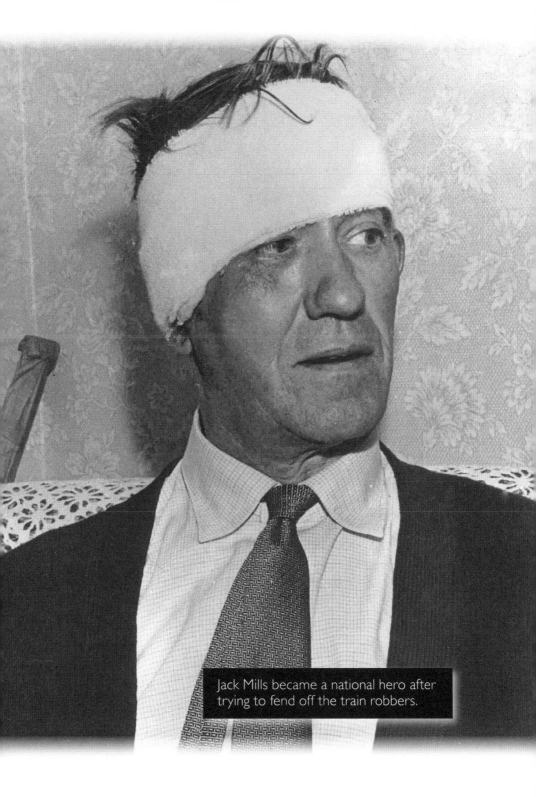

Jack Mills became a national hero after trying to fend off the train robbers.

THE POSTAL WORKERS WERE SHOCKED WHEN AN AX-WIELDING MAN CAME CRASHING THROUGH A WINDOW OF THE CAR.

The first sign of trouble was a man's voice outside the car. Though the man was talking about guns, the robbers didn't have any. However, the weapons they did have were frightening enough. The postal workers were shocked when an ax-wielding man came crashing through a window of the car. He was followed by a rush of men through the door. The postal workers knew they couldn't fight off the robbers.

As the postal workers were subdued, Mills and Whitby, handcuffed together, were forced to lie on the embankment near the train tracks. Whitby saw an army truck and a Land Rover on the road below the bridge. He watched helplessly as the masked robbers formed a human chain to move the mailbags from the train to the waiting truck.

With the loot loaded, the robbers forced Mills and Whitby into the HVP car. Before leaving, the robbers warned the men not to move. One look at Mills' bloody and battered face proved to everyone in the HVP car that the robbers' threats should be taken seriously.

CHAPTER 5

THE PLAN BREAKS DOWN

Speeding away from Bridego Bridge, Bruce Reynolds was quietly content. Some of the other robbers couldn't contain their glee and excitement. Reynolds recalled that men in the second getaway car laughed as they sang along with a popular radio tune, "It's the Good Life!" It was a feeling they all shared.

As far as any of them knew, only one problem had threatened their criminal plan, and it had been solved quickly. When their train driver, Stan, had fumbled with the brakes and controls, the robbers had replaced him with Jack Mills. Told he would get "some more stick" if he did not cooperate, Mills reluctantly had driven from Sears Crossing to Bridego Bridge. Heading toward Leatherslade Farm, Stan was probably the only worried man among the robbers. He wondered whether his criminal associates would kill him for his failure.

As the robbers pulled into the farm's driveway at 4:30 a.m., their special radio picked up a police announcement: "You won't believe this, but they've stolen a train."

While the robbers were hurrying to their hideout, the victims of their crime were beginning to move. About 15 minutes after the heist, Dewhurst climbed out of the HVP train car. Seeing no robbers, he sent two workers to phone police from the nearest farm. Dewhurst didn't know the robbers had cut phone lines nearby. At Sears Crossing, train guard Frank Miller climbed out of his train car to see what was causing the delay. He headed toward the engine for information. He was amazed to see that the engine and first two cars were missing.

Miller returned to his car and followed standard safety procedures. He set up red lanterns 1,000 yards (914 m) behind the last car of the stalled train. These warning lights would prevent an oncoming train from crashing into the night mail cars. Then the guard headed back up the track until he reached Bridego Bridge and the victims there. They waved down and got aboard a train traveling on another track. At the next station, they phoned news of the theft to village police. These officers called London's Scotland Yard, which in turn phoned the Buckinghamshire County police. The announcement heard by the robbers was probably an alert sent out at about that time to officers on patrol.

The first police to search the crime scene were local ones. There was little physical evidence at the site of the robbery: a bloodstained cloth, a dropped cap, and some broken links that had held train cars together. No train worker had gotten a clear view of any of the robbers' faces. David Whitby was the only

Police found a crowbar near Bridego Bridge while investigating the robbery.

one who knew more. He told police he had seen an army truck and a Land Rover. He also said he thought one of the robbers spoke with a Cockney accent.

Even at a distance, experts at Scotland Yard were helpful. Learning that one robber had warned the victims not to move for half an hour, George Hatherill, the deputy assistant commissioner of Scotland Yard's Flying Squad, drew an important conclusion. He decided that the robbers' hideout must be within a half-hour of Bridego Bridge. That was a logical reason for mentioning that amount of time in a warning.

Hatherill was right. His suggestion that police search for isolated buildings within a half-hour's drive of Bridego Bridge narrowed the hunt to an area with a radius of about 30 miles (48 km) from the bridge. Thus on August 13, Hatherill's insight into a thoughtless remark led police to Leatherslade Farm. The search might have taken more time, however, if the robbers had been able to understand the views of people unlike themselves.

THE FLYING SQUAD OF SCOTLAND YARD

The large Metropolitan Police Force based in London is often called Scotland Yard. The name comes from its original 19th century headquarters, which stood near buildings that once housed kings and other important visitors from Scotland. Now the New Scotland Yard is located elsewhere in the city, but the nickname has stuck.

The famous Flying Squad of Scotland Yard was started in 1918. Its detectives were given special vehicles and drivers to investigate major crimes and catch criminals throughout London. The nickname "flying squad" came from their ability to move quickly from place to place. Because the squad's detectives have special knowledge of the criminal underworld and major crimes, other police sometimes ask for their help on big cases.

A police car escorted the truck and Land Rovers police believed were used in the robbery.

These big-city criminals didn't understand the friendly curiosity of farmers in small communities. The robbers also didn't realize that their own precautions would place them in danger. A neighboring dairy farmer, John Maris, had seen heavy new curtains in Leatherslade Farm's windows. He wondered why, even in the daytime, only the corners were ever pulled open. Someone might peek out, but no one could see inside the farmhouse. When he later noticed a truck in the farm's shed and its locked garage, Maris remembered the news about the nearby train robbery. Maris thought Leatherslade Farm might be the hideout police were trying to find. He phoned local police with his suspicions. The police, though, were being flooded with more than 400 leads in the case. It took another day and another phone call from Maris before they set out to investigate Leatherslade.

In the meantime, the robbers' moods had changed dramatically. At first, after counting the cash, they had celebrated their huge heist. They jumped up and down and even lit cigarettes with old pound notes. Some of the robbers began playing Monopoly—using real money. Then news of a search in the area for an isolated building with army vehicles was reported to the public. While Maris was puzzling over Leatherslade Farm, the alarmed robbers speeded up their schedule.

"THE WHOLE PLACE IS ONE BIG CLUE."

They had planned to leave Leatherslade during the weekend. Instead, some left Thursday, and the rest left Friday. Distrusting one another, they had rejected the idea of using a nearby airfield for a quick getaway. Instead of flying the loot or themselves away all at one time, they divided the cash and left the farm one by one. Some waited for rides from associates such as Brian Field. Bruce Reynolds claims to have strolled onto a country road and walked until he was given a lift by two men. Reynolds said he even had an enjoyable conversation with the men about the terrible train robbery.

Before they left Leatherslade, the gang burned empty mailbags in the yard. Their attempts to clean up their trash were not thorough because someone had been hired for this vital task. Various accounts say Buster Edwards, Gordon Goody, Brian Field, or another robber hired the cleaner to come right away. One account says the cleaner was hired to burn down the buildings. Whatever the agreement, the gang paid this mysterious figure as much as 40,000 pounds (U.S. $112,000) for this urgent job.

Yet when police reached Leatherslade Farm, they found the hideout intact and filled with the robbers' belongings. Buckinghamshire Detective Malcom Fewtrell remarked that "the whole place is one big clue." Food, dishes, clothes, pound notes, and the abandoned Monopoly game lay where the rushed robbers had left them. The criminals' fingerprints were on some of the items.

Except for Goody, many of the robbers had abandoned their plan of always wearing gloves while at Leatherslade. The August heat had made the gloves too annoying or uncomfortable. A couple of

Mailbags found at Leatherslade Farm were
unloaded at a police station.

the robbers had tried wrapping their fingertips in
bandages to avoid leaving fingerprints. Heat and
friction, though, usually made the bandages fall off.
Yet the robbers hadn't worried much about leaving
fingerprints. They had expected that the cleaner
would erase any trace of their time at the farm.

Within 10 days Scotland Yard had identified
several of the robbers. Its crime lab had matched
fingerprints left at Leatherslade to ones already
on file.

Detectives and historians disagree about why the cleaner didn't do his job. He may have been a traitor who betrayed the robbers by not cleaning or burning their hideout. Or he might have had an accident before he could complete his task. Yet it seems clear that the robbers' own casual remarks and acts before they fled Leatherslade helped police to track and capture some of them. Sheer luck and the robbers' poor choices led Scotland Yard's finest to most of the other criminals—some much sooner than others.

CHAPTER 6

CAPTURE AND TRIAL

S cotland Yard sent some of its best detectives to track down the robbers. Detective Chief Superintendent Tommy Butler was in charge of the case. The 50-year-old veteran of the police force worked harder than anyone else in the Flying Squad. During his career Butler was officially praised 32 times for "brilliant work in detection." Detective Inspector Frank Williams, who became detective chief superintendent after Butler, knew the habits of London's major criminals better than any other officer. Detective Leonard "Nipper" Read became a police legend for his pursuit and capture of brutal gang leaders. Detective John "Jack" Slipper, later another detective chief superintendent, also helped bring the robbers to justice.

Yet none of their knowledge and experience was needed to nab the first train robber to be caught. Within a few days, bad luck led to Roger Cordrey's arrest. After leaving Leatherslade Farm, he had contacted an old friend named Bill Boal. Without explaining why, Cordrey told Boal that

he needed to hide from the police. Boal agreed to
help. The two men tried to rent a garage at a private
home. But when they offered to pay in cash, with a
large bundle of 10-shilling notes, the owner, Ethel
Clarke, became suspicious. The widow of a police
sergeant, she had heard all about the train robbery.
She contacted the police, who caught Cordrey and
Boal in her garage. After police found about 140,000
pounds (U.S. $392,000) hidden in their belongings,
both men were charged as robbers. Boal protested
his innocence, but police did not believe him.

Within 10 days fingerprint evidence had
identified Charlie Wilson and Ronnie Biggs. Wilson
had handled a salt shaker and a first-aid kit at the
farm, and Biggs had touched a ketchup bottle. They
were the next to be arrested. According to some
accounts, Wilson taunted arresting officer Tommy
Butler. He supposedly said that he didn't believe
Butler could make the robbery charges stick without
having the money from the heist. Wilson allegedly
added, "[A]nd you won't find that."

Ronnie Biggs under arrest in Britain

Bad luck ruined the alibi Biggs had previously
planned. Charmain Biggs thought her husband was
away chopping wood during the heist. When Biggs'
brother unexpectedly died, she asked the police
to find her husband and give him the news. Police
couldn't find Biggs anywhere near where his wife
believed him to be, which destroyed his alibi.

"I FELT POSITIVE THAT WHAT WE HAD FOUND WAS A SPECIALLY PREPARED SOFT-LANDING SPOT FOR A LEAP FROM THE ROOF."

Bruce Reynolds, Buster Edwards, James White, John Daly, Tommy Wisbey, Jimmy Hussey, and Roy James also had left fingerprints at Leatherslade Farm. James' prints were on a dish he had used to feed a stray cat. Hussey had left his palmprints and fingerprints on the gang's truck. No fingerprints were found for Goody, but police suspected he had been involved because of his past connections with the others. Within the next two months, the Flying Squad found Wisbey and Hussey without much trouble. Capturing the athletic James took a little longer.

James had gone into hiding once the hunt for Wilson had become news. But Detective Jack Slipper received word about James' inner-city hideout. Before trying to arrest him, Slipper located possible escape routes in nearby alleys and backyards. He found a freshly dug area near a garbage heap. "I felt positive," he said later, "that what we had found was a specially prepared soft-landing spot for a leap from the roof." It was completely different, the detective added, from the "pieces of broken bottles and bits of twisted metal that lay everywhere else." Slipper stationed an officer there—and found out he was right. After a long chase up staircases and across rooftops, James jumped down 30 feet (9 m) onto the spot Slipper had targeted. The waiting officer arrested him. Police later found about 12,000 pounds (U.S. $33,600) among James' belongings.

Though Goody had not left fingerprints at the farm, the police lab later matched yellow paint on a pair of his shoes to paint found at the farm. It had been used to try to disguise the army truck. The match was used as evidence to arrest Goody. A few historians question whether Goody would have left the paint on his shoes. They agree with Reynolds,

who said the police planted the evidence to have
a reason to arrest him. Reynolds later wrote, "I
knew that Tommy Butler would make sure that the
evidence was conclusive. … [H]e simply took short
cuts which he saw as legitimate." But no evidence
supports that claim. Chance events had destroyed
the alibi Goody had prepared for himself. He had
left a false trail to show that he was in Ireland at a
family gathering during the heist. But the gathering
had ended early because of a family quarrel.

Reynolds, Edwards, and White still eluded
police. However, they caught Daly in downtown
London. And after tracing the purchase of
Leatherslade Farm, police also arrested Brian Field,
Lennie Field, and John Wheater, among others,
and accused them of being accomplices. Brian Field
was also linked to the robbery by a receipt in one of
four loot bags found in Dorking Woods, just south
of London. Police didn't solve the mystery of why
the bags, containing a total of more than 100,000
pounds (U.S. $280,000), had been abandoned there.

Nor did they figure out who had left more than 47,000 pounds (U.S. $131,600) in a phone booth the night James was captured. A friend of James' might have had the money and panicked. Detectives had differing theories but no proof.

Police recovered very little of the stolen 2.6 million pounds (U.S. $7 million). That fueled the government's desire to capture all the robbers and find all of the stolen money. Their desire was strengthened by newspaper accounts. Headlines praised the daring and cunning of the robbers, while cartoons mocked the police. One cartoon showed Detective Malcom Fewtrell, magnifying glass in hand, stooping to follow a trail of pound notes. They were falling from a sack carried by a robber.

The trial of those captured in connection with the robbery began January 20, 1964. It was held in a poorly heated and crowded town hall in Aylesbury, a town northwest of London. Coughs and the smell of damp wool filled the air. More than 200 witnesses testified. They included train driver Jack Mills, who spoke about his injuries. There were so many records of the investigation and the trial that— placed side by side—they occupy 8 feet (2.4 m) of shelf space in Britain's National Archives.

Scotland Yard's Tommy Butler outside court in Aylesbury

The trial lasted until April 16, making it at the time the longest criminal trial in British history.

But one verdict was given before the trial ended. John Daly was acquitted in February. Since the only evidence against him was his fingerprints on pieces of the Monopoly game, the judge said there was "no more than suspicion" against Daly. He could have handled the Monopoly tokens and board before the robbery. One of those arrested got off lightly. John Wheater, who was in charge of the office where lawyer Brian Field worked, got three years in prison.

Most of the robbers who had been at Bridego Bridge during the heist were sentenced to 30 years in prison. Cordrey, the only robber to plead guilty, was sentenced to 20 years. Boal, still protesting his innocence, got 24 years.

Brian Field and Lennie Field were sentenced as accomplices to 25 years. The men were stunned by the length of their punishment, since in England not even murderers received such long sentences.

Some members of the public also questioned the severity of the punishment. Later Reynolds wrote

WERE THE SENTENCES FAIR?

Newspaper reporters and observers wondered about the fairness of imprisoning most of the robbers for 30 years when some murderers only got five-year terms. One headline blasted, "30 YEARS—ALL BRITAIN ARGUES, IS THIS TOO HARSH?"

The judge explained the long sentences in his opening remarks:

This is nothing more than a sordid crime of violence which was inspired by vast greed. The motive of greed is obvious. As to violence, anybody who has seen that nerve-shattered engine driver can have no doubt of the terrifying effect on law-abiding citizens of a concerted assault by armed robbers. To deal with this case leniently would be a positively evil thing. Potential criminals who might be dazzled by the enormity of the prize must be taught that the punishment they risk will be proportionately greater.

Detective Jack Slipper later said, "I've always been convinced that it was only by chance that there wasn't more violence" committed during the train robbery. His view echoes those of people who think the robbers deserved harsh prison sentences.

about the apparent unfairness of the British court system. He noted that thief John Daly had been acquitted while Bill Boal had been convicted. "If the train driver Jack Mills was the victim of our crime," Reynolds declared, "then Bill Boal was the victim of the judicial process."

In August 1964 an appeals court judge refused to reduce the sentences of the robbers who had pleaded "not guilty." He did lower the sentences of Brian Field, Lennie Field, Roger Cordrey, and Bill Boal. Brian Field's and Lennie Field's prison time was reduced to five years each. Cordrey's and Boal's sentences were reduced to 14 years each. Even this amount of time, though, was longer than typical in Britain for robbery. The long prison sentences influenced decisions made by the robbers who still eluded capture. The fear of long prison terms also influenced the choices of two convicted robbers. Soon newspaper headlines would again shout the names of Wilson and Biggs.

CHAPTER 7

LIFE ON THE RUN

*S*till on the run, Bruce Reynolds, Buster Edwards, and James White knew that capture or surrender would lead to long prison terms. Reynolds and Edwards first secretly went to France, where Edwards had plastic surgery to change his appearance. In 1964 and 1965, the men and their wives used fake passports and escaped separately to Mexico. June Edwards traveled there with her elementary school-age daughter. Friends of the Reynolds family brought 2-year-old Nick Reynolds to Mexico. By that time, he didn't recognize his father.

In a way, the robbers' families became victims of the crime too. This was the case with White's family, who had remained in hiding in Britain. White, his wife, Sheree, and their 6-month-old son first lived in a motor home. White hid much of his loot in its walls. After the Whites had to flee the home, police found the money there. To better hide from the police, the Whites left their son with a paid caregiver. White and his wife were apart from their son for about a year. When they reclaimed the boy,

"TAKE A GOOD LOOK AT THEM AS THEY WILL BE OVER THE WALL SOON."

he was ill and dirty. White never explained why he surrendered so easily to police early in 1966. Yet his remark then to Detective Jack Slipper suggests his state of mind. He said, "Look ... if you'll just look after Mum [his wife] and the kid, I'll give you no trouble at all." White was sentenced to 18 years in prison. His sentence indicates that the judge thought the 30-year sentences had been too harsh.

While Reynolds, Edwards, and White were trying to go unnoticed, Charlie Wilson and Ronnie Biggs made headlines. In separate, daring escapes, they broke out of prison. At their sentencing, Butler had predicted this would happen. Looking at the gloomy, stunned robbers, Butler had said to another officer, "Take a good look at them as they will be over the wall soon."

Terrible prison conditions increased Wilson's desire to risk a prison break. Winson Green Prison, built in the 1840s, was designed for 350 prisoners, but 800 men were crammed inside its grim gray walls. During the day Wilson's job was—in a bitter twist of fate—sewing canvas mailbags. At night his cell was lighted, which kept him from getting restful sleep. Wilson claimed that prison guards beat him. When a friend contacted Wilson with an escape plan, he eagerly accepted.

On August 12, 1964, a team of men from the outside broke Wilson out of prison. The team included a locksmith and mountaineers. They had rehearsed their plan at an old monastery in France. Its high stone walls were like the ones at Winson Green Prison. Another prisoner worked with them, using a smuggled walkie-talkie to tell the team when guards went by. After scaling the walls and opening Wilson's cell, the men helped him climb to freedom. Wilson sped away from prison hiding inside a specially outfitted oil tanker. Instead of fuel, its large cylinder contained a mattress, pillows, and blankets.

Wilson's escape made Biggs' life in old Wandsworth Prison even harder. Like Wilson, Biggs had been assigned to sew mailbags and was kept in a constantly lighted cell. Now, to prevent another prison break, guards moved Biggs between cells at night. One guard was always outside his cell. The light, frequent cell changes, and noisy guard made sleep almost impossible for Biggs. He tried to clean his cell, but each time he was moved into another dirty, bug-filled one. Biggs later said he had planned to serve his time and work toward parole, but prison conditions had changed his mind. Biggs accepted his friends' offer to help him escape.

On July 8, 1965, men in a red furniture van drove up to Wandsworth Prison. About one-third of the van's roof had been cut away. The vehicle was equipped with an elevator that raised the men so they could climb to the top of the 25-foot (7.6-m) prison wall. Then they lowered a mountaineering ladder to the prison yard. Biggs climbed the ladder and went over the wall. He jumped down through the van's open roof onto a mattress the men had placed there to ensure a soft landing. Then Biggs ran to a waiting car and fled. His escape took him to Antwerp, Belgium, where he had plastic surgery and secured a fake passport. He then traveled to

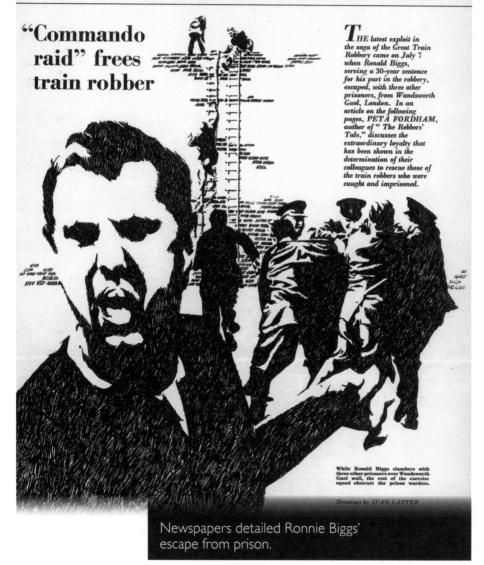

SATURDAY, JULY 17, 1965

THE ILLUSTRATED LONDON NEWS.

© 1965. THE ILLUSTRATED LONDON NEWS & SKETCH LTD.   The World Copyright of all the Editorial Matter both Illustrations and Letterpress, is Strictly Reserved.   No. 6572—Volume 247

"Commando raid" frees train robber

THE latest exploit in the saga of the Great Train Robbery came on July 7 when Ronald Biggs, serving a 30-year sentence for his part in the robbery, escaped, with three other prisoners, from Wandsworth Gaol, London. In an article on the following pages, PETA FORDHAM, author of "The Robbers' Tale," discusses the extraordinary loyalty that has been shown in the determination of their colleagues to rescue those of the train robbers who were caught and imprisoned.

While Ronald Biggs clambers with three other prisoners over Wandsworth Gaol wall, the rest of the exercise squad obstruct the prison warders.

Drawings by IVAN LAPPER

Newspapers detailed Ronnie Biggs' escape from prison.

Australia. His wife and elementary school-age sons secretly joined him there later.

Life on the run worked out differently for Edwards and Reynolds. Though Reynolds was happy living abroad, Edwards was not. Edwards and his wife, June, had never traveled far from London. Living in Mexico, learning a new culture, and trying to learn Spanish were too hard. The health problems of their daughter Nicole increased their unhappiness. In 1966 the Edwards family returned to England. In September 1966 Edwards was arrested. About three months later, he was sentenced to 15 years in prison.

Reynolds, on the other hand, continued to enjoy life in Mexico. He and his family also traveled to and lived in a grand mansion in the south of France. For almost five years after the train robbery, they

"IT'S NO LIFE FOR ANYONE, ALWAYS DRIFTING ABOUT."

lived lavishly. Then Reynolds returned to Britain with his family. He was concerned about how his associates were handling his money. He also may have been a little homesick. On November 8, 1968, Scotland Yard's Tommy Butler surprised Reynolds at his comfortable rented house. When Butler arrested him, Reynolds admitted the strain of the years of avoiding arrest. "I'm glad it's over," he said. "It's no life for anyone, always drifting about. … I had been thinking for some time about giving myself up."

At Reynolds' trial, in January 1969, the judge was not lenient. Saying Reynolds had enjoyed "the fruits of [his] crime" for five years, the judge concluded that "living with the fear of … arrest" did not justify a light sentence for the robber. He sentenced Reynolds to 25 years in prison.

Reynolds' capture was Butler's second recent triumph. In early 1968 Butler had finally nabbed Wilson, who had been living with his wife, Pat, and three young daughters in a small town in Canada.

Calling himself Ronald Alloway, Wilson had become a successful businessman and respected member of his community. Yet his family had lived with constant tension and fear. Wilson and his wife had trained their daughters to answer to false names. The Wilsons kept a secret safe filled with cash inside their home for a quick getaway. After Wilson was arrested, his wife admitted to feeling relieved.

"The strain, the tension, it all went. I still had things to worry about, but I could begin to live a normal life again," she said.

Police found 30,000 pounds (U.S. $84,000) in Wilson's home. Wilson was sentenced to 30 years. He was sent to Pentonville Prison, where several of the other train robbers were also imprisoned.

Butler had delayed retiring from the police force to capture these robbers. Now, of the known train robbers, only Biggs remained free. But this small-time crook turned out to be the most elusive of all. Before he was finally captured and sent back to prison, Biggs became known as the most wanted man in the world.

Using fake names, Biggs and his family lived quietly in Australia until 1969. He worked as a carpenter while Charmain Biggs did factory work. They needed the jobs because much of his loot had been spent to flee Britain. In addition, another criminal had charged Biggs 10,000 pounds (U.S. $28,000) to change all his white five-pound notes into newer, less noticeable blue ones. Fearing capture, Biggs often abruptly moved his family from one city to another. His wife complained, saying, "If only you'd never got involved in the train robbery, we wouldn't have to live like nomads. Life with you is one disaster after another." She did not realize that worse was yet to come.

In 1970 Biggs escaped capture by leaving his family and fleeing to South America. Charmain Biggs then had to support and raise her sons by herself. Using the name Michael Haynes, Biggs settled in Brazil. He took odd jobs. In 1974 Detective

Even though he was a fugitive, Ronnie Biggs lived like a celebrity in Brazil.

Jack Slipper almost managed to bring Biggs to justice. But Brazilian laws stopped him. Similar laws kept bounty hunters from returning Biggs to Britain in 1981. Biggs became a well-known figure in Brazil. Tourists went out of their way to meet him. When Biggs' autobiography was published in 1994, he was pleased with his notoriety. He wrote, "I don't expect to be pardoned and to be perfectly honest I don't want to be. Stop being Ronnie Biggs? You must be joking!" The next 10 years, however, brought enormous changes for Biggs.

SELLING THE STORY

Some people profited from the story of the train robbery and its aftermath. Brian Field's German-born wife sold articles about the crime to German newspapers. After Charlie Wilson's capture, his wife received 30,000 pounds (U.S. $84,000) for her tale. A 1968 British newspaper headline announced, "MRS. CHARLIE WILSON TELLS THE LOT-SCOOP OF THE YEAR."

When Ronnie Biggs abandoned his family in Australia, his wife needed money. She sold family photos as well as details of their life in hiding. A British newspaper paid her 65,000 pounds (U.S. $182,000) for the photos and her story. Seven of the robbers earned money from a 1975 book written by Piers Paul Read. The sale horrified the widow of train driver Jack Mills. "You can imagine my feelings," she told an interviewer, "when I hear the robbers are being paid money for their story, as though they did something splendid and brave. They ruined the life of a good, hard-working man."

In 1981 Biggs sold his life story to a British newspaper. Both Biggs and Bruce Reynolds profited from the books they later wrote. In addition, in 1999 they served as paid consultants for a company that was making a video game based on the robbery.

CHAPTER 8

THE ROBBERS' FATES

Over the years movies, TV specials, books, and newspaper and magazine articles have kept the train robbers in the public eye. A 1967 British film called *Robbery* was based on what came to be called "The Crime of the Century" and "The Great Train Robbery." The film isn't a documentary, but it features similar acts set in a fictional story.

A 1988 movie, *Buster*, showed Buster Edwards' involvement in the heist. It starred popular musician Phil Collins as Edwards. *Buster* features comedy as well as drama. The film ends with the family's return to England and Edwards' capture. In 2006 a British TV documentary focused on the failed 1981 attempt to bring Ronnie Biggs back to Britain. It contains an interview with one of the bounty hunters who briefly held Biggs captive.

Yet none of these accounts is fully accurate or complete. The fate of the robbers is more complicated than any of these portraits. Even the autobiographies written by some of the robbers are incomplete. Some of the stories conflict with one another—and with the public record. However, there is no doubt that their participation in the robbery changed the courses of their lives. Each of them was affected in a different way. Some of the robbers became law-abiding, while others turned back to crime. Edwards could not tolerate his life after prison and committed suicide.

Accomplices Brian Field and John Wheater were the first to be released from prison. Wheater moved to another part of Britain. Field vanished from public sight. His name appeared in newspapers again only when he died in a 1979 car crash. Bill Boal died of cancer in 1970, while still in prison. Seven of the robbers were paroled in 1975, after having served 10 years of their prison sentences. They worked out a story to sell to publishers, and told their tale to author Piers Paul Read, who wrote *The Train Robbers*. Then the former gang members separated.

James White ran a painting business. Roger Cordrey went back to being a florist. Bob Welch became a car dealer and gambler. He had become lame in prison because officials had delayed a knee operation. Later the surgery went wrong.

Gordon Goody moved to Spain, where he bought and ran a bar. Jimmy Hussey worked at a market stall and opened a restaurant. Tommy Wisbey ran a bar. In 1989 Hussey and Wisbey went to prison again, this time for dealing drugs.

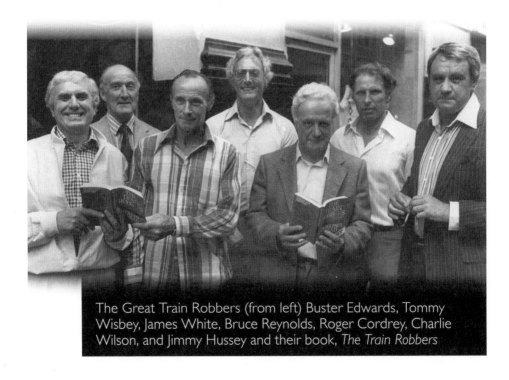

The Great Train Robbers (from left) Buster Edwards, Tommy Wisbey, James White, Bruce Reynolds, Roger Cordrey, Charlie Wilson, and Jimmy Hussey and their book, *The Train Robbers*

At first Roy James worked as a silversmith, a trade he had learned in prison. When Charlie Wilson was released from prison in 1978, the two men went into business together. In 1983 they were arrested for cheating on their taxes. Later Wilson

SOUVENIRS OF THE GREAT TRAIN ROBBERY

Is a five-pound note ever worth 1,800 pounds? The answer is yes—if the money was part of the loot from the Great Train Robbery. In a November 2007 auction, a buyer paid that much for a stolen note, along with photos belonging to the family of a detective who worked on the case. The detective said the government had let him keep the souvenir. The buyer probably valued the note so highly because the Great Train Robbery remains fascinating even today.

The whereabouts of most of the loot, if it has not all been spent, is still unknown. So are the identities of some of the robbers.

"YOU NEVER STOP MISSING THE BUZZ."

moved to Spain, where he became heavily involved in dealing drugs. In April 1990, on his 35th wedding anniversary, Wilson was mysteriously murdered in his home. No one was ever arrested for the murder, which was probably related to Wilson's drug deals.

In 1993 James was again in prison. During a family quarrel, he had beaten his ex-wife and had shot her father. Both of the victims lived, but James died in 1997 after suffering a heart attack.

Edwards hanged himself in 1994. Even though the movie *Buster* concludes with cheerful music and rueful smiles, Edwards wasn't happy. Working as a flower seller, he may have had money problems. He might have been depressed because he thought the police were closing in on him. Boredom might have been a factor as well. Bruce Reynolds said both he and Edwards had become criminals more for the excitement than for the monetary rewards. "You never stop missing the buzz," Reynolds said.

After his release in 1978, Reynolds was unable to stay away from crime. Caught with illegal drugs in 1983, he was sentenced to three years in prison. After serving that time, Reynolds finally became law-abiding.

It is Ronnie Biggs, however, who has been most recently in the news.

By 2001 Biggs, then 71 years old, had had three strokes and was partly paralyzed. He also was homesick. He returned to Britain hoping to receive a pardon. Instead the notorious robber was imprisoned for the rest of his long sentence. Train driver Jack Mills' son was just one person who opposed pardoning Biggs. "I resent those who have made money from my father's death," John Mills said.

Detective Chief Inspector Jack Slipper also opposed Biggs' release. Slipper died in 2005.

In August 2009, because Biggs seemed near death, he was finally released from a prison hospital. He was moved to a nursing home near his son.

There are still unsolved mysteries about the Great Train Robbery. One is the number of people who were involved in the crime. It's clear that the robbers received inside information about night mail schedules and procedures from a railroad employee. This unknown person—the Ulsterman—was never caught. The robbers might have had more than one informant or inside helper. It's even uncertain how many criminals were at Sears Crossing on August 8, 1963.

Police later identified 12 robbers at Sears Crossing that night, yet files in the British National Archives show that police thought 15 to 17 men were there. Several have never been identified or caught. Detective Inspector Frank Williams later noted with disgust, "At least three men who were directly involved are still at liberty and enjoying to the full their share of the money stolen and the profits from the way they invested it. One of them is responsible for the attack on the train driver." Reynolds and

Biggs also maintain that one of several unidentified robbers beat Mills.

The Great Train Robbery had a direct impact on British railroad regulations. After the robbery, train drivers were no longer permitted to leave their engine cabs after stopping for red signals. They had to keep their cab doors locked. Yet the change no longer helps to prevent railroad thefts, since night mail trains stopped running in 2004.

Today vast sums of money are more likely to be transported—and stolen—electronically. Former businessman Bernie Madoff, who could be called another great robber, was sentenced in 2009 to 150 years in prison for stock fraud. He stole more than $65 billion—and he didn't even have to leave his office to commit the crime.

THE FATE OF DRIVER JACK MILLS

Long after the Great Train Robbery, driver Jack Mills continued to feel dizzy and have headaches. There were questions about whether his injuries had caused his lingering symptoms. Though Mills died of leukemia in 1970, some people believed the injuries he suffered during the robbery hastened his death.

Most people agreed that his reward for resisting the robbers was shamefully small. Even though he never worked as a train driver again, the railroad company gave him just 250 pounds (U.S. $700). Yet it offered a reward of 10,000 pounds (U.S. $28,000) for information about the thieves or their loot. When Charmain Biggs later sold her story for 65,000 pounds (U.S. $182,000), Mills' condition again became news.

In 1970 a British newspaper ran a campaign to raise money for Mills. People donated a total of 34,000 pounds (U.S. $95,200)—enough for him and his wife to buy a small house just before he died.

TIMELINE

August 8

1963

A night mail train is robbed north of London, and the robbers escape with about 2.6 million pounds (about U.S. $7 million).

August 13

1963

Police find the robbers' hideout at Leatherslade Farm.

January 20

1964

The trial of the train robbers who have been captured begins.

February 11

1964

John Daly is acquitted in the robbery.

April 16
1964
The train robbers are sentenced to prison.

August 12
1964
Charlie Wilson escapes from prison.

July 8
1965
Ronnie Biggs escapes from prison.

April 12
1966
James White is captured.

TIMELINE

September 19
1966
Buster Edwards is arrested.

December
1967
Wilson is recaptured.

November 8
1968
Bruce Reynolds is arrested.

1970
Ronnie Biggs flees from Australia to Brazil; Charmain Biggs is paid for her story; and the public donates money to a fund for train driver Jack Mills.

1975
Seven of the robbers are released from prison.

1994
Buster Edwards commits suicide.

May 2001
Ronnie Biggs returns to Britain voluntarily.

August 9 2009
A seriously ill Biggs is released from prison.

GLOSSARY

accomplice—person who helps someone else carry out a plan, particularly an illegal one

acquitted—judged not guilty of a crime

alibi—evidence that a person accused of a crime was somewhere else when the crime was committed

archives—collection of documents and records of historical interest

blackjack—short, leather-covered club used as a weapon

Cockney—native of the working-class East End of London; the accent of East Enders

diesel—engine that burns a type of heavy mineral

front man—person used to hide the identity of another who is really in control

lenient—inclined to show mercy rather than being harsh or strict

locksmith—someone who makes or repairs locks

notoriety—fame gained because of a bad act or quality

parole—supervised early release of a prisoner for good behavior or other reasons

police-band radio—radio that receives signals broadcast on frequencies used only by police and other emergency responders

prosecute—to bring legal action to punish someone who has broken the law

silversmith—someone who makes or repairs items made of silver

stock—ownership share in a business

walkie-talkies—hand-held radio transmitters and receivers

ADDITIONAL RESOURCES

READ MORE

Editors of *Life* magazine. *Life: Greatest Unsolved Mysteries of All Time*. New York: Life Books, 2009.

McCaughrean, Geraldine. *Britannia: 100 Great Stories From British History*. London: Orion Children's Books, 2004.

Newton, Michael. *The Encyclopedia of Unsolved Crimes*. New York: Facts on File, 2009.

INTERNET SITES

Use FactHound to find Internet sites related to this book. All of the sites on FactHound have been researched by our staff.

Here's all you do:
Visit *www.facthound.com*
Type in this code: 9780756543600

SELECT BIBLIOGRAPHY

Biggs, Ronald. *Odd Man Out: My Life on the Loose and the Truth About the Great Train Robbery*. London: Bloomsbury, 1994.

Clarkson, Wensley. *Killing Charlie: The Bloody, Bullet-Ridden Hunt for the Most Powerful Great Train Robber of Them All*. London: Mainstream Publishing, 2004.

Delano, Anthony. *Slip-Up: Fleet Street, Scotland Yard, and the Great Train Robbery*. New York: Quadrangle/New York Times Book Co., 1975.

Fordham, Peta. *The Robbers' Tale: The Real Story of the Great Train Robbery*. New York: Popular Library, 1965.

Gray, Mike, Ted Currie, and Michael Biggs. *Ronnie Biggs: The Inside Story*. Essex, England: Apex Publishing Ltd., 2009.

Green, Michelle, and Meg Grant. "A Quarter Century After His Great Train Robbery, Ronald Briggs Isn't Railing at Life on the Lam." *People*. 10 Oct. 1988. 1 May 2010. www.people.com/people/archive/article/0,,20100161,00.html

Guttridge, Peter. *The Great Train Robbery*. Surrey, England: The National Archives, 2008.

Mackenzie, Colin. *Biggs, The World's Most Wanted Man*. New York: W. Morrow, 1975.

Magee, Julie. "Historic Fiver's Up for Sale." *Daily Echo.*
1 Nov. 2007. 1 May 2010. www.bournemouthecho.co.uk/
news/1800494.Historic_fiver____s_up_for_sale/

Pace, Eric. "Ronald (Buster) Edwards, Great Train Robber."
The New York Times. 5 Dec. 1994. 1 May 2010.
www.nytimes.com/1994/12/05/obituarites/ronald-buster-
edwards-great-train-robber.html

Read, Piers Paul. *The Train Robbers.* New York: Avon Books, 1978.

Reynolds, Bruce. *The Autobiography of a Thief.* London:
Virgin Publishing Ltd., 2000.

Slipper, Jack. *Slipper of the Yard.* London: Sidgwick &
Jackson, 1981.

Williams, Frank. *No Fixed Address: Life on the Run for the
Great Train Robbers.* London: W.H. Allen, 1973.

Wilson, Jamie. "After 35 years, Biggs is Back in Jail." *The
Guardian.* 8 May 2001. 1 May 2010. www.guardian.co.uk/
uk/2001/may/08/jamiewilson

INDEX

arrests, 17, 53–54, 56–58, 61, 71, 72–73, 79, 82

Biggs, Charmain, 55, 74, 77, 87
Biggs, Ronald, 18, 21, 26, 54, 55, 63, 67, 68–69, 73–74, 76, 77, 79, 84, 85–86
Boal, Bill, 53–54, 61, 63, 80
Bridego Bridge, 25, 27, 36, 41, 42, 44, 61
Buster (movie), 79, 83
Butler, Tommy, 53, 54, 58, 67, 72, 73

Clarke, Ethel, 54
Cordrey, Roger, 21, 24, 30, 53–54, 61, 63, 80

Daly, John, 27, 30, 56, 58, 61, 63
Dewhurst, Frank, 11, 36, 42

Edwards, June, 65, 71
Edwards, Nick, 65
Edwards, Nicole, 71
Edwards, Ronald "Buster," 18, 19, 21, 23, 24, 49, 56, 58, 65, 71, 79, 80, 83

Fewtrell, Malcom, 49, 59
Field, Brian, 23, 27, 28, 48, 49, 58, 61, 63, 77, 80
Field, Lennie, 28, 58, 61, 63

Flying Squad, 44, 45, 53, 56

Goody, Gordon "Footpad," 18, 19, 21, 23, 24, 49, 56, 57, 58, 81

Hatherill, George, 44
High Value Package (HVP) car, 9, 10, 11, 15, 31, 36, 39, 42
Hussey, Jimmy, 18, 31, 56, 81

James, Jesse, 20
James, Roy, 18, 19, 25, 26, 30–31, 56–57, 59, 82, 83
Jennings, Bill, 31

Kett, Thomas, 11, 36

Leatherslade Farm, 23, 27, 28, 41, 44, 46–48, 49–51, 53, 56, 58

Madoff, Bernie, 86
Maris, John, 46–47
Miller, Frank, 42
Mills, Jack, 15, 33, 35–36, 39, 41, 60, 63, 77, 84, 86, 87
Mills, John, 84

night mail trains, 9, 10, 11, 12, 17, 23, 28, 33, 36, 85, 86

Porter, Edwin, 20

Read, Leonard "Nipper," 53
Read, Piers Paul, 77, 80
Reynolds, Bruce "The Major," 17, 18, 19, 21, 23, 24, 25, 26, 27, 28, 30, 41, 48, 56, 57–58, 61, 63, 65, 67, 71–72, 77, 83–84, 85–86
Robbery (film), 79

Scotland Yard, 42–43, 44, 45, 50, 51, 53, 72
Sears Crossing, 12, 25, 30, 33, 41, 42, 85
signal lights, 24, 25, 30, 33, 42, 86
Slipper, John "Jack," 53, 56–57, 62, 67, 74, 76, 84
"Stan," 26, 41

"Ulsterman," 23, 85

Welch, Bob, 31, 80–81
Wheater, John, 28, 58, 61, 80
Whitby, David, 15, 33, 35, 39, 43–44
White, James, 28, 56, 58, 65, 67, 80
White, Sheree, 65
Williams, Frank, 53, 85
Wilson, Charlie, 17, 18, 19, 21, 23, 28, 54, 56, 63, 67–68, 72–73, 77, 82–83
Wilson, Pat, 72, 73, 77
Wisbey, Tommy, 18, 24, 56, 81

ABOUT THE AUTHOR

Brenda Haugen started in the newspaper business and had a career as an award-winning journalist before finding her niche as an author. Since then, she has written and edited many books, most of them for children. A graduate of the University of North Dakota in Grand Forks, Brenda lives in North Dakota with her family.